Practice

Mc Graw Hill Education

Bothell, WA • Chicago, IL • Columbus, OH • New York, NY

Cover: Nathan Love

www.mheonline.com/readingwonderworks

Send all inquiries to:
McGraw-Hill Education
Two Penn Plaza
New York, New York 10121

ISBN: 978-0-02-129947-8
MHID: 0-02-129947-1

Printed in the United States of America.

5 6 7 8 9 RHR 17 16 15 14

A

CONTENTS

Unit 1

CONTENTS

Unit 2

Unit 3

CONTENTS

Unit 4

Unit 5

CONTENTS

Unit 6

Name _____

Say the first two picture names. Listen for the beginning sound. Say the last two picture names. Circle the picture whose name has the same beginning sound.

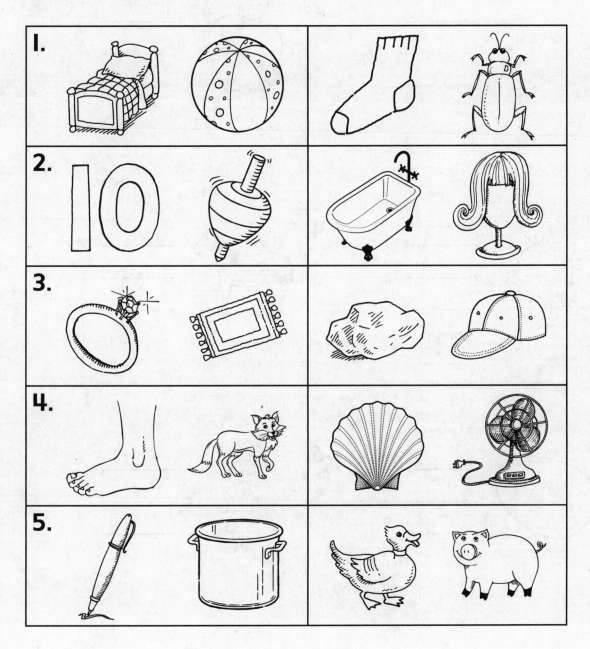

Name _____

Say each picture name. Write the letter that stands for the sound you hear at the beginning of its name.

1.  _____
- - - - - -
_____

2.  _____
- - - - - -
_____

3. 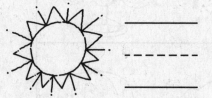 _____
- - - - - -
_____

4.  _____
- - - - - -
_____

5. 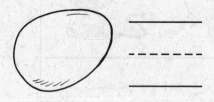 _____
- - - - - -
_____

6.  _____
- - - - - -
_____

Name _____

Say each picture name. Write the letter that stands for the sound you hear at the beginning of its name.

1. 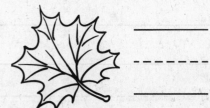 _____

2.  _____

3. 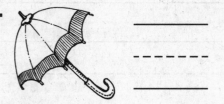 _____

4. 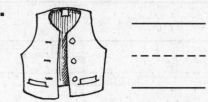 _____

5. 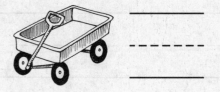 _____

6. 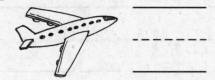 _____

Name _____

Read the word. Spell and trace the word. Then write the word.

1.

2.

3.

4.

5.

6.

I can juggle.

Comprehension: Which of the activities would you like to do? Why?

At Home: Ask your child to read the book aloud to you.

I Can!

I can jump.

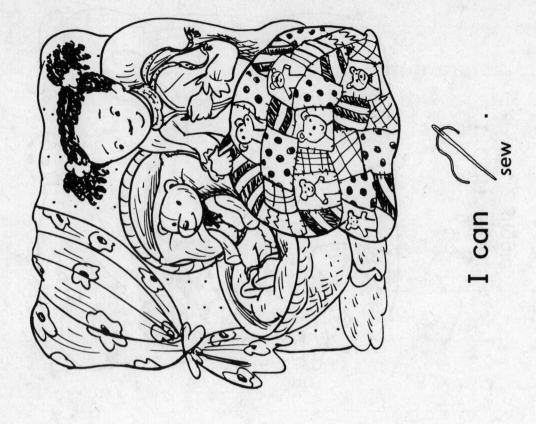

I can  <u>sew</u>

High-Frequency Words: Circle the words
<u>I</u> and <u>can</u> in the story.

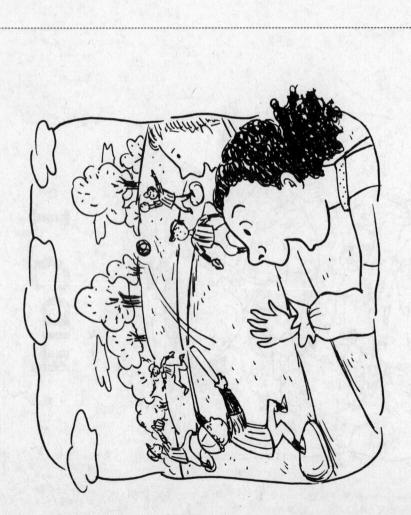

I can  yell

Name _____

Say each picture name. Circle the picture if its name begins with the same sound you hear at the beginning of *ax*.

Name _____

c<u>a</u>p

Say each picture name. Circle the picture whose name has the short <u>a</u> sound in the middle. Write <u>a</u> under the picture.

1.

_____   _____

- - - - - - -   - - - - - - -

_____   _____

2.

_____   _____

- - - - - - -   - - - - - - -

_____   _____

3.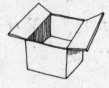

_____   _____

- - - - - - -   - - - - - - -

_____   _____

4.

_____   _____

- - - - - - -   - - - - - - -

_____   _____

5.

_____   _____

- - - - - - -   - - - - - - -

_____   _____

Name _____

Say the picture name. Fill in the missing letter for each word. Then trace the word.

1.  p _ d

2. 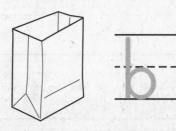 b _ g

3. 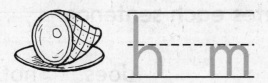 h _ m

4. 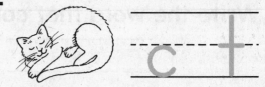 c _ t

5. 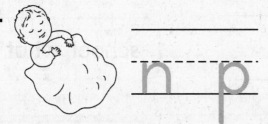 n _ p

6. 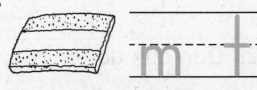 m _ t

7.  v _ n

8.  h _ t

Name _____

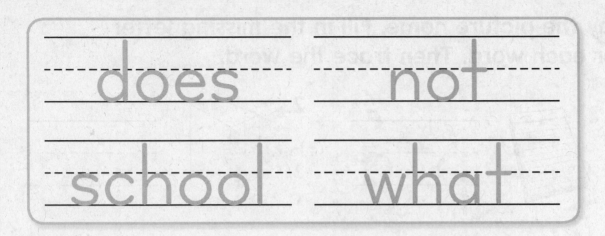

Write the word that completes each sentence.

1. This is _____ my bag.

does   not

2. Dan can go to _____.

school what

3. Mac _____ quack.

not   does

4. Can you see _____ this is?

school what

Sam does not tap.

High-Frequency Words:
Circle the words does
and not in the story.

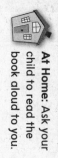

At Home: Ask your
child to read the
book aloud to you.

Does Sam Tap?

Can Hal tap, tap, tap?

Does Sam tap?

Comprehension: What is Hal making?

Hal can tap, tap, tap.

Phonics: Circle the words in the story that have the **short _a_** sound.

Name _____

Say each picture name. Place an X on the picture whose name has a different middle sound.

1.

2.

3.

4.

5.

Name _____

bib

Say each picture name. Circle the word that names each picture.

1.  fan

   fin

2.  pig

   pack

3.  lid

   lad

4.  pan

   pin

5.  wig

   wag

6.  hat

   hit

Name _____

Read each word. Then spell and trace the word. Then draw a line from the word to the picture it names.

1.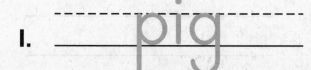

2.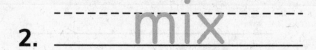

3.

4.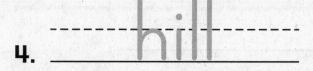

5.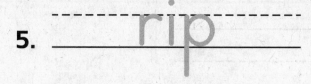

6. six

Name _____

Read each word. Trace and spell each word.
Write the word on the line.

1. 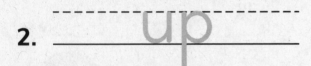 _____   _____

2. 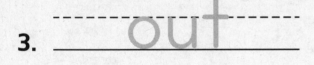 _____   _____

3.  _____   _____

4. _____   _____

---

1.  See it go _____!

2.  It is _____.

3.  Sam is _____ sad.

Comprehension: Where did Jim hit it?

At Home: Ask your child to read the book aloud to you.

Jim hits it out!

Hit It Out!

Liz will hit it.

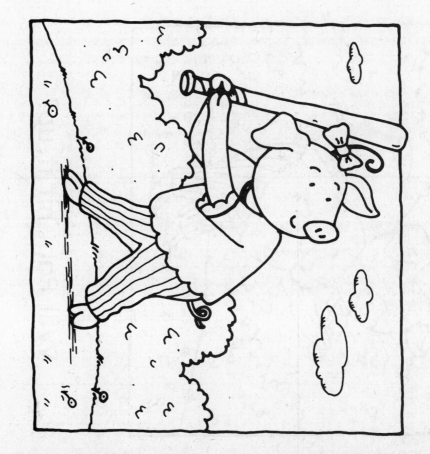

Where will Jim hit it?

High-Frequency Words: Circle the words up and out in the story.

Will Pam hit it up?

Phonics: Circle two names in the story that have the short *i* sound. Circle a word that rhymes with it.

Name _____

Say each picture name. Look at the first picture, then circle the two pictures whose names have the same middle sound.

1.			
2.			
3.			
4.			
5.			
6.			

Name _____

glass

Say each picture name. Pick the letters that complete each word. Circle them and write them.

1.

_____
- - - - - - -
_____ag

fl   bl

2.

_____
- - - - - - -
_____am

pl   cl

3.

_____
- - - - - - -
_____ad

gl   fl

4.

_____
- - - - - - -
_____ap

cl   gl

5.

_____
- - - - - - -
_____ick

sl   pl

Name _____

Write the letters on the line to make a word. Read the word. Then circle the picture the word names.

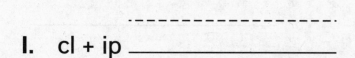

_____

- - - - - - - - - - - - - - - - -

1. cl + ip _____

_____

- - - - - - - - - - - - - - - - -

2. sl + am _____

_____

- - - - - - - - - - - - - - - - -

3. cl + ap _____

_____

- - - - - - - - - - - - - - - - -

4. fl + ip _____

_____

- - - - - - - - - - - - - - - - -

5. cl + iff _____

Name _____

Read each word. Then spell and trace the word. Then write the word.

1. 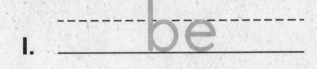 _____

2.  _____

3.  _____

4. 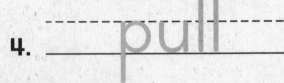 _____

Write the word from the box that means the opposite.

5. bad _____

6. go _____

pull   good

come   be

Six pigs are glad pigs!

High-Frequency Words:
Circle the words good
and come in the story.

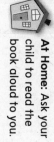

At Home: Ask your child to read the book aloud to you.

Six Glad Pigs

Kids see pigs at Flat Slats.

Six pigs come sip.

Comprehension: Where does the story take place?

Bliss pats six good pigs.

Phonics: Circle words in the story with fl, bl, and gl.

Name _____

Say each picture name. Listen to the middle sounds. Place an X on the picture whose name has a different middle sound.

1.

2.

3.

4.

5.

Name _____

h<u>o</u>p

Read each word. Say each picture name.
Draw a line to the word. Then trace the word.

1.

2.

3.

4.

5.

6.

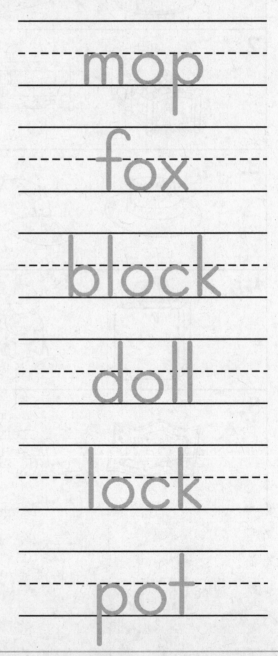

mop

fox

block

doll

lock

pot

Name _____

clock	hog	socks
rod	box	log

Write a word from the box to name each picture.

1.
_____
- - - - - - - - - - - - - - -
_____

2.
_____
- - - - - - - - - - - - - - -
_____

3.
_____
- - - - - - - - - - - - - - -
_____

4.
_____
- - - - - - - - - - - - - - -
_____

5.
_____
- - - - - - - - - - - - - - -
_____

6.
_____
- - - - - - - - - - - - - - -
_____

Name _____

Read each word. Spell each word. Then trace each word.

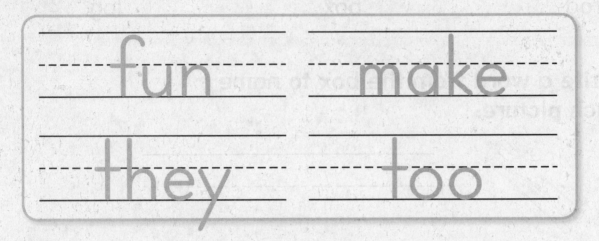

Read each sentence, Circle the correct word. Write the word on the line.

1. We have _____.

   | fun | they |

2. _____ play with us.

   | They | Too |

3. She is six, _____.

   | make | too |

4. I will _____ it.

   | fun | make |

They nap in a big log.

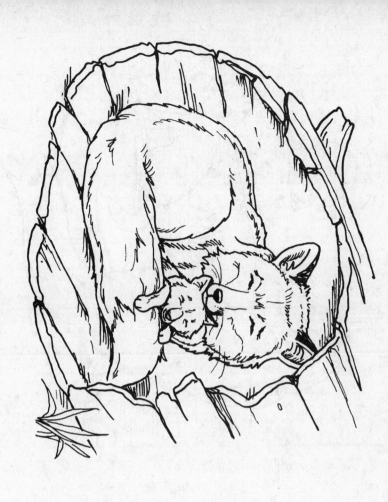

High-Frequency Words:
Circle the words too and
They in the story.

At Home: Ask your
child to read the
book aloud to you.

Fox Fun

Mom fox licks Tom fox.

Tom fox hops on it, too.

Mom hops on a flat rock.

Name _____

Say each picture name. Listen for the beginning sounds in each picture name in the row. Put X on the word that has different beginning sounds.

Name _____

crab

stick

Read each word. Circle the picture it names.

1. frog

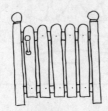

2. swim

3. track

4. grass

5. drill

6. smock

Name _____

Say the picture name. Fill in the missing letters for each word. Then trace the word.

1.  _____ ill

2.  _____ og

3.  _____ ib

4.  _____ in

5.  _____ op

6.  _____ ick

7.  _____ ick

Name _____

A. Read each word. Then spell and trace the word.

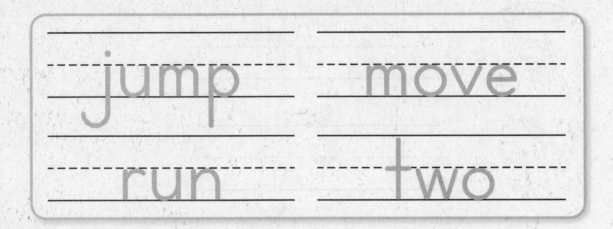

B. Circle the word that completes each sentence. Then write the word on the line.

1. Here are _____ cats.

   two   run

2. Can you _____ this box?

   two   move

3. I _____ to school.

   two   run

4. We _____ up and down.

   jump   two

A crab can swim, swim, swim.

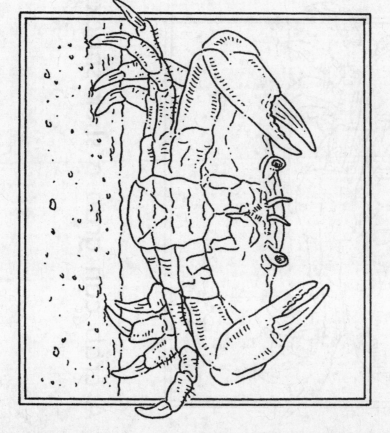

High-Frequency Words:
Circle the word Move in the story.

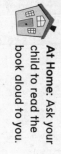

Crab on the Move

A crab can move.
Click, clack, click.

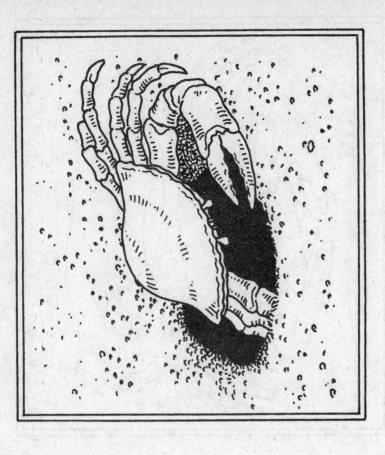

A crab can dig.
It can dig big pits.

Comprehension: What can a crab do with its claws?

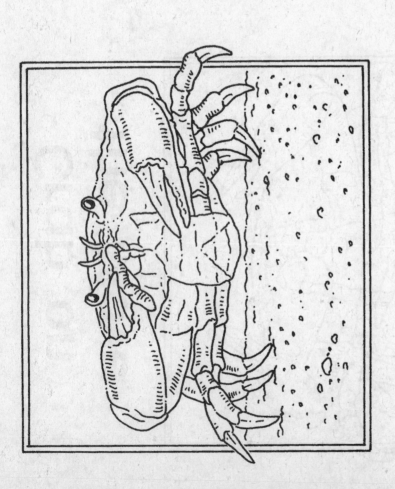

A crab can grab a slick snack.

Phonics: Circle words in the story with cr, gr, or sw.

Name _____

Say each picture name. Listen for the middle sound. Draw a line to a picture whose name has the same middle sound.

1.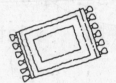

2.

3.

4.

5.

Name _____

n<u>e</u>t

br<u>ea</u>d

Say each picture name. Circle the word that names each picture.

I.    jot

jet

2.    well

will

3.    pan

pen

4.   bad

bed

5.    ten

tan

6.    hid

head

Name _____

Write a word from the box to name each picture.

vet	bread	web
stem	bell	hen

1.  _____

2. _____

3.  _____

4.  _____

5.  _____

6.  _____

Name _____

A. Read each word. Spell and trace each word.

1.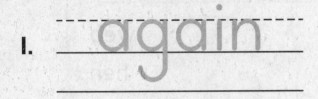

2.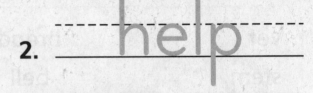

3.

4.

5.

B. Write a word from above to complete each sentence.

6. I have a _____ pet cat.

7. I _____ fins to swim.

8. I _____ to make a snack.

Rex's vet will help his leg.
It will get well again!

High-Frequency Words:
Circle the words <u>help</u>,
<u>use</u>, <u>there</u>, <u>new</u>, and
<u>again</u> in the story.

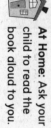

At Home: Ask your
child to read the
book aloud to you.

Rex Gets Help

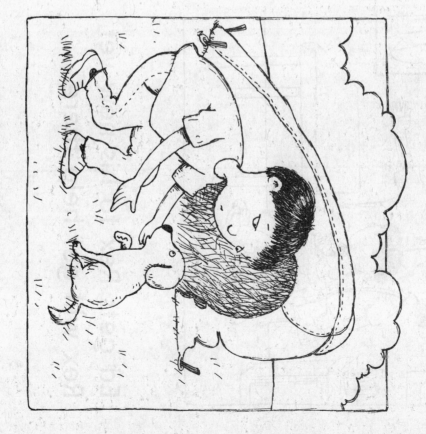

Rex is Ed's pet.
Rex can not use his leg.

The vet pats Rex's head.
Rex licks his vet.

Comprehension: Why does Ed take Rex to the vet?

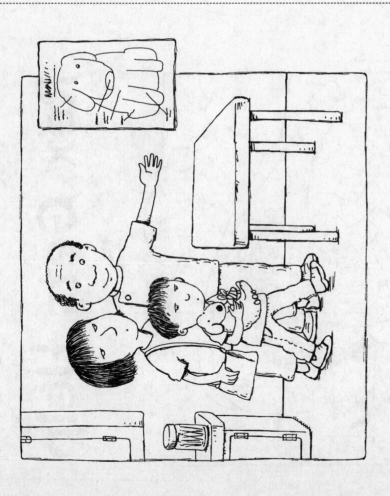

Ed gets Rex to his new vet.
Rex will get help there.

Phonics: Circle the words in the story that have the sound in the middle of vet.

Name _____

Say the picture names in the row. Circle the picture whose name has the same middle sound as the first picture in the row.

1.			
2.			
3.			
4.			
5.			

Name _____

dr**u**m

Say each picture name. Write u next to the picture if its name has the short u sound.

1. 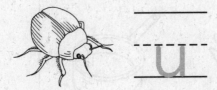   u

2.

3.

4.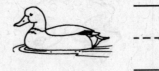

5.

6.

7.

8.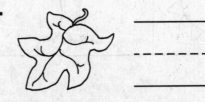

Name _____

A. Circle the word that names the picture.

1.  bag
bug

2. truck
track

3. cap
cup

4. pup
pop

B. Say the word that names the picture. Write the missing letter. Trace the word.

5.  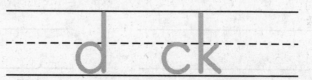 d _ ck

6.  s _ n

7.  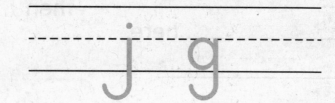 j _ g

Name _____

A. Read the word. Then spell and trace the word. Then write the word.

1.  _____

2. 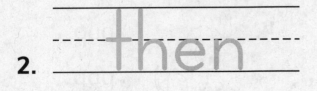 _____

3. 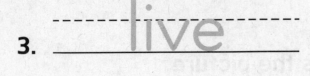 _____

4. 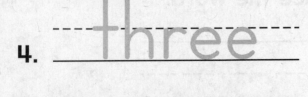 _____

5.  _____

B. Write the word from the box that completes each sentence.

6. I _____ here. | then   live |

7. We _____ go. | could   one |

Practice • Grade I • Unit 2 • Week 3

High-Frequency Words:

Circle the words <u>one</u> and <u>then</u> in the story.

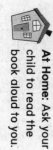

At Home: Ask your child to read the book aloud to you.

Then Duck gets wet.

Duck

Duck runs!

Duck is one big mess.

Comprehension: Who are the characters in the story?

Duck jumps in the mud.

Phonics: Circle words in the story that have the **short u** sound.

Name _____

Say each picture name. Listen for the end sounds in each picture name in the row. Put X on the picture whose name does not have the same end sounds.

1.			
2.			
3.			
4.			
5.			

Name _____

ant

Say each picture name. Trace and read each word. Then draw a line to the word.

1.

pond

2.

desk

3.

cast

4.

stamp

5.

tent

6.

skunk

Name _____

Write the letters on the line to make a word. Read the word. Then circle the picture the word names.

_____

- - - - - - - - - - - - - - - -

1. ba + nk _____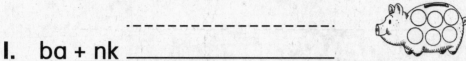

_____

- - - - - - - - - - - - - - - -

2. ve + st _____

_____

- - - - - - - - - - - - - - - -

3. ma + sk _____

_____

- - - - - - - - - - - - - - - -

4. la + mp _____

_____

- - - - - - - - - - - - - - - -

5. pla + nt _____

Name _____

A. Read each word. Then spell and trace the word.

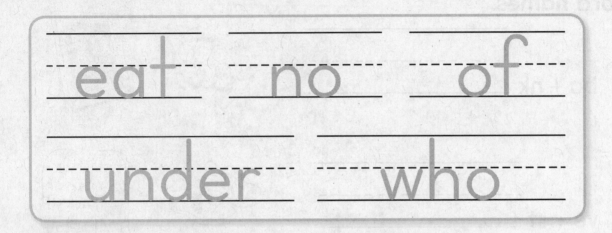

B. Write a word from the box above to complete each sentence.

1. I see _____ is here.

2. There is _____ dust under this bed.

3. She is one _____ my pals.

4. We like to _____ clams.

Kits just fit in a den of sand.
Kits must rest for a bit.

High-Frequency Words:
Circle the words of, no, and Who in the story.

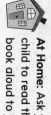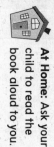 **At Home:** Ask your child to read the book aloud to you.

Den of Sand

Six kits run, jump, and bump.
No kit stops to eat and rest.

Kits spot a den of sand.
Can six kits fit in a den?

Comprehension: Why do the kits need to rest?

Who will get to a den last?
One kit must run very fast.

Phonics: Circle words in the story that end with nd, mp, and st.

Name _____

Say the picture name. Listen for the beginning sound. Say each picture name below. Put a ✓ in the box for each picture name that has the same beginning sound.

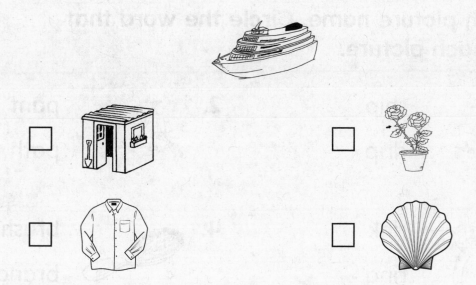

Say the picture name. Listen for the end sound. Say each picture name below. Put a ✓ in the box for each picture name that has the same end sound.

Name _____

fi<u>sh</u> wi<u>ng</u> ba<u>th</u>

Say each picture name. Circle the word that names each picture.

1.  ship

drip

2.  pant

path

3.  rink

ring

4.  brush

brand

5.  flash

trash

6.  shell

spell

Name _____

Say each picture name. Circle the letters and write them to complete the word.

1.
_____
- - - - - - -
____ed

sl   sh

2.
_____
- - - - - - -
di____

sh   ng

3.
_____
- - - - - - -
ba____

th   nk

4.
_____
- - - - - - -
ki____

ck   ng

5.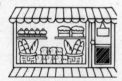
_____
- - - - - - -
____op

st   sh

6.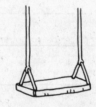
_____
- - - - - - -
swi____

sh   ng

Name _____

A. Read each word. Spell and trace the word.

1. _____ all

2. _____ call

3. _____ day

4. _____ her

5. _____ want

B. Read each clue. Write a word from above to match it.

6. to wish for _____

7. to yell out _____

8. in the sun _____

Seth sets a ship in the tank.
The fish want to swim to it.

Comprehension: How does Seth get the fish to swim?

At Home: Ask your child to read the book aloud to you.

A Ship for All?

Seth has a fish shop.
His fish swim in tanks.

Seth thinks in his shop.
Then Seth brings a ship.

Seth sits in his shop all day.
Seth thinks of the fish.

Name _____

Say the picture name. Then say the sounds in the word, one at a time. Draw one dot in each box for each sound you hear. Write the number of sounds.

1.  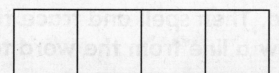 _____

2. 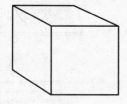 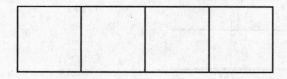 _____

3.  _____

4.  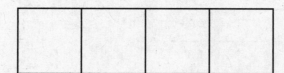 _____

5.  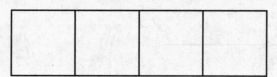 _____

Name _____

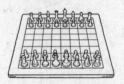

check	latch	whale	phone

Read each word. Then spell and trace the word. Then draw a line from the word to the picture it names.

1. _chick_

2. _whip_

3. _chess_

4. _branch_

5. _pitch_

6. _bench_

Name _____

Write a word from the box to name each picture.

lunch	whiz	fetch
switch	chop	match

1.

_____

- - - - - - - - - - - - - - - - - - -

_____

2.

_____

- - - - - - - - - - - - - - - - - - -

_____

3.

_____

- - - - - - - - - - - - - - - - - - -

_____

4.

_____

- - - - - - - - - - - - - - - - - - -

_____

5.

_____

- - - - - - - - - - - - - - - - - - -

_____

6.

_____

- - - - - - - - - - - - - - - - - - -

_____

Name _____

A. Read each word. Spell and trace each word. Then write the word.

1.  _____

2. _____

3. _____

4. _____

5. _____

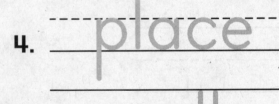

B. Draw a line from each word to its meaning.

6. many   • next to

7. walk   • lots of things

8. by   • take steps

Chuck and Kim set dishes.

They set lunch on the dishes.

It is a picnic on checks.

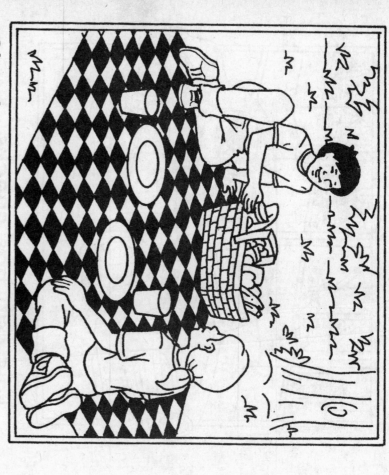

High-Frequency Words:
Circle the words <u>around</u>,
<u>many</u>, <u>by</u>, and <u>walk</u> in
the story.

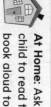

At Home: Ask your
child to read the
book aloud to you.

Checks
All Around

Which things have checks?
This flag has many checks.

This cab has checks.
It stops by a shop. Dad
and Meg walk. Then they
catch the cab.

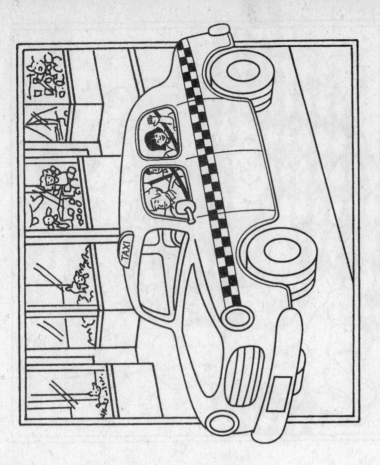

Steph and Dad play on
checks. Steph is a whiz at it.
Steph is a champ with chips
on checks.

Comprehension: Where can you
find checks?

Phonics: Circle words in the story with
ch, tch, wh, and ph.

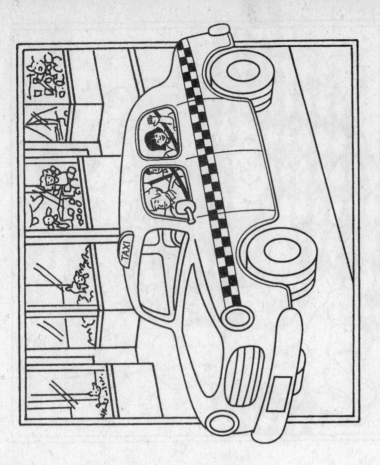

③

②

Name _____

Say the two picture names. Listen for the same middle sound. Draw a line to a picture whose name has the same middle sound.

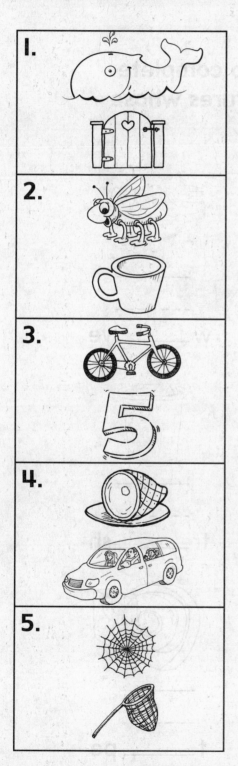

Name _____

__r__**a**__k__**e**

Say each picture name. Write __a__ to complete each picture name. Circle the pictures whose names have the long __a__ sound.

1.

_____

- - - - - - -

m_____sk

2.

_____

- - - - - - -

w_____ve

3.

_____

- - - - - - -

c_____ke

4.

_____

- - - - - - -

tr_____sh

5.

_____

- - - - - - -

fr_____me

6.

_____

- - - - - - -

t_____pe

Name _____

Say each picture name. Circle the word that names each picture.

1.
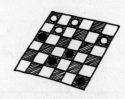

game   gas

2.

vase   vast

3.

man   mane

4.

flag   flame

5.

snake   snack

6.

gaps   grapes

Name _____

A. Read each word. Then spell and trace the word.

1. 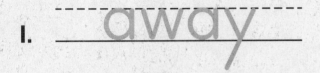 away

2. 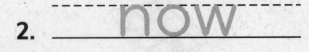 now

3.  some

4. 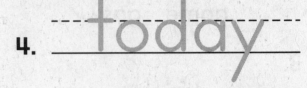 today

5. 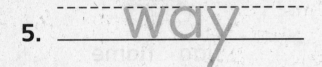 way

6. 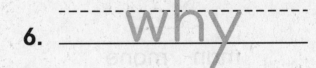 why

B. Read each clue. Write a word to match it.

7. this day

8. not then

9. not here _____

Now Jake munches on grapes.
Jane munches on red grapes.
Yum! Yum! Yum!

High-Frequency Words:
Circle the words today,
some, and now in
the story.

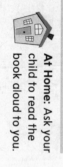

At Home: Ask your
child to read the
book aloud to you.

Have Some Grapes

Jake and Jane are pals.
Today Jake and Jane walk
on the lane.

Jake makes fun shapes
with grapes.
Jane makes fun shapes with
grapes, too.

Jake can get some big
plates. Jane fills them with
red grapes.

Name _____

Directions: Say the picture name. Then say the sounds in the word, one at a time. Place one marker in each box for each sound you hear. Write the number of sounds.

I.  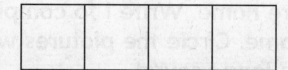 _____

2.  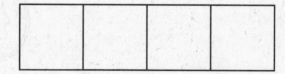 _____

3.  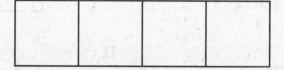 _____

4.  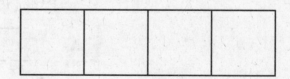 _____

5.  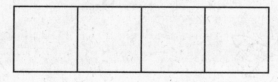 _____

Name _____

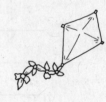

bike

Say each picture name. Write __i__ to complete each picture name. Circle the pictures whose names have the long __i__ sound.

1.

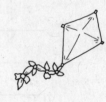

_____

- - - - - - -

k_____te

2.

- - - - - - -

d_____me

3.

_____

- - - - -

f_____sh

4.

_____

- - - - - -

h_____ve

5.

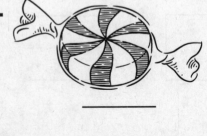

_____

- - - - - - -

m_____nt

6.

_____

- - - - - - -

sl_____de

Read each word. Circle the picture it names.

1. lime

2. hike

3. vine

4. pipe

5. smile

6. prize

Name _____

A. Read each word. Then spell and trace the word.

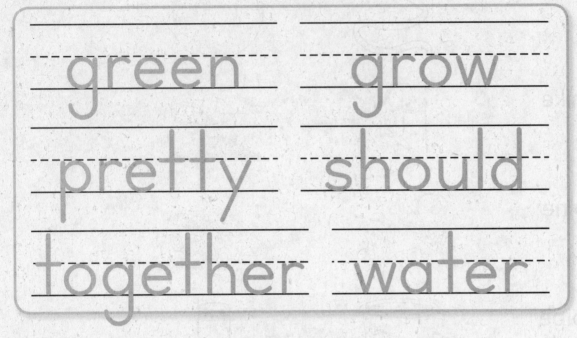

green   grow

pretty   should

together   water

B. Write a word from above to complete each sentence.

_____
- - - - - - - - - - - - - -

1. I drink _____.

_____
- - - - - - - - - - - - - -

2. Plants can _____.

_____
- - - - - - - - - - - - - -

3. Grass is the color _____.

Mike made it! He is quite wet, but he is on time.

Mike and Miss Fine can dine together at five.

High-Frequency Words:
Circle the words should, water, and together in the story.

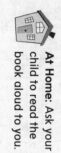

At Home: Ask your child to read the book aloud to you.

Let's Dine Together

Miss Fine invited Mike to dine.

They will dine at five.

Mike gets set with a big smile.

Mike spots a lake. He dives in.
Mike swims a mile in the
water. Will he make it to
Miss Fine's?

Comprehension: What is Mike's problem?
How does he solve it?

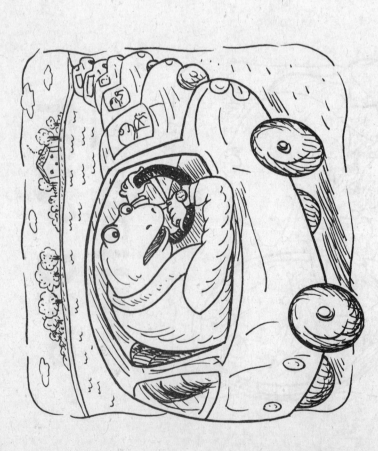

Mike gets stuck in line.
He still has a mile to drive.
What should Mike do?

Phonics: Find five words in the story that
have the long *i* sound.

Name _____

Follow the directions from your teacher.

1.

2.

3.

4.

5.

Teacher Directions: Say the following sounds. Have children blend the sounds to say each word and then circle the picture that shows it. I. /f/ /e/ /n/ /s/; 2. /k/ /ā/ /j/; 3. /j/ /e/ /m/; 4. /m/ /ī/ /s/; 5. /s/ /t/ /ā/ /j/

Name _____

 page   **laces**   **hedge**

Say each picture name. Draw a line to the word. Then trace and read the word.

1.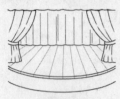

2.

3.

4.

5.

6.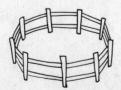

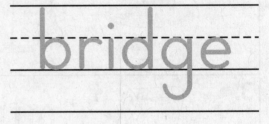

bridge

rice

stage

face

badge

fence

Name _____

Read the word. Take away the first letter or letters. Add the new letter and write the new word. Then draw a picture to show the word.

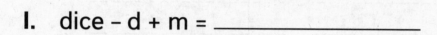

1. dice – d + m = _____

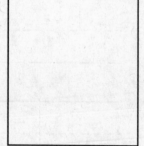

2. page – p + c = _____

3. ledge – l + w = _____

4. chance – ch + d = _____

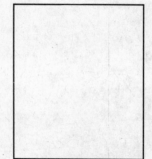

Name _____

A. Read each word. Then spell and trace the word.

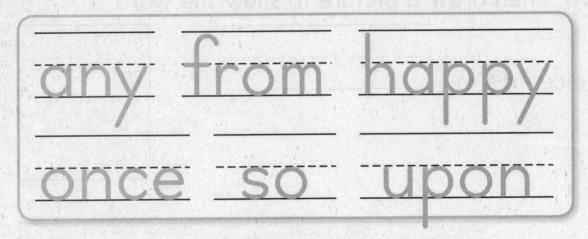

B. Choose a word from above to complete each sentence in the story.

_____

Once _____ a time Ike was sad. He did

not have _____ pals. Then Ike met Matt

at school. Now Ike is very _____!

race prize.

Grace is so happy with her

Mom smiles at Grace.

"I got wet!" states Mom.

High-Frequency Words:
Circle the words from, so,
and happy in the story.

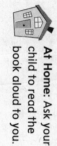

At Home: Ask your
child to read the
book aloud to you.

Happy Grace
Wins the Race

Grace's race has ended.
Grace rests on the edge.
"Nice race, Grace!"
Mom states.

Grace swam at a fast pace.
She raced best in her class.
Grace gets a prize from
the judge. "It is nice to
win," thinks Grace.

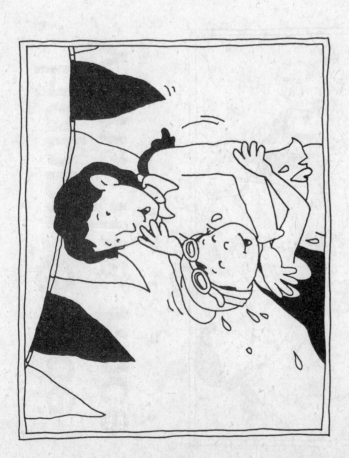

Grace hugs Mom.
"Did I win?" asks Grace.
"Let's check with the judge,"
states Mom.

Name _____

Say the picture name. Listen for the middle sound. Circle the picture in the row whose name has the same middle sound.

1.			
2.			
3.			
4			
5.			

Name _____

b<u>o</u>ne

m<u>u</u>le

Read each word. Then spell and trace the word. Then draw a line from the word to the picture it names.

1. mole

2. rose

3. note

4. cube

5. stove

6. dune

Name _____

Say the picture name. Fill in the missing letter for each word. Then write the word on the line.

1. r____be   _____

2. m____le   _____

3.  h____se   _____

4. p____le   _____

5.  t____be   _____

6. ph____ne   _____

7. gl____be   _____

8. fl____te   _____

Name _____

A. Read each word. Then spell and trace the word.

1. _____ ago

2. _____ boy

3. _____ girl

4. _____ how

5. _____ old

6. _____ people

B. Write a word from above to complete each sentence.

7. How _____ is that girl?

8. The boy lived long _____.

How could Cub get in that hole?
"I am huge, but I fit. Thanks, Mole," said Cub.

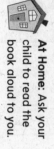

Comprehension: How does Mole help Cub?

At Home: Ask your child to read the book aloud to you.

Cub and Mole's Hole

Cub got wet. "Look, an old hole. It is not wet in that hole." Cub said.

"I do not wish to be rude, but it is wet. Can I fit in, Mole?" asked Cub.

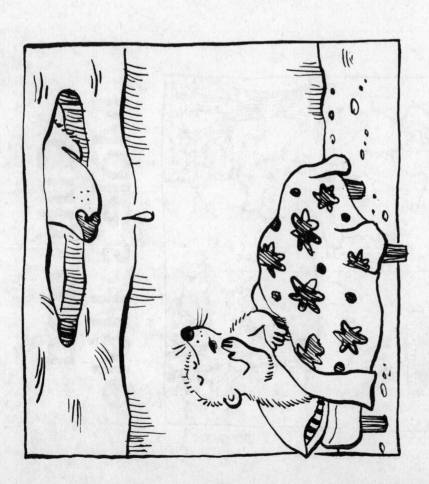

Cub poked his nose inside. Mole slept in his bed. A drop woke Mole up.

Name _____

Blend the sounds your teacher says to form a word. Circle the picture that shows the word.

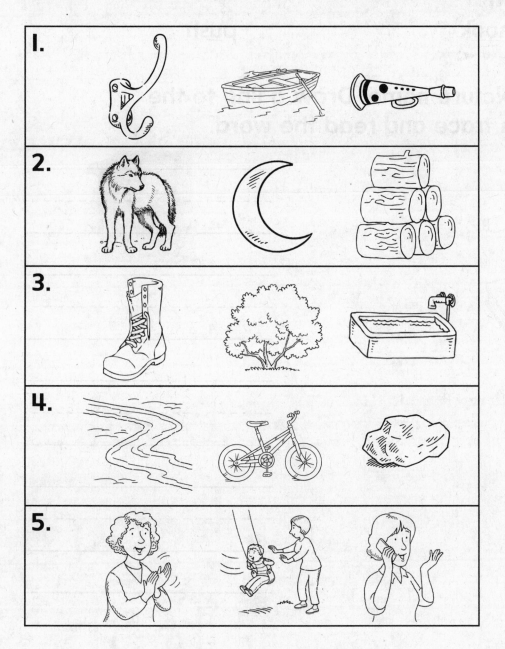

Teacher Directions: Listen as I say the following sounds. Blend the sounds to say each word and then circle the picture that shows it. I. /h/ /ù/ /k/; 2. /w/ /ù/ /d/; 3. /b/ /ù/ /sh/; 4. /b/ /r/ /ù/ /k/; 5. /p/ /ù/ /sh/

Name _____

 h<u>oo</u>k   p<u>u</u>sh

Say each picture name. Draw a line to the word. Then trace and read the word.

1.    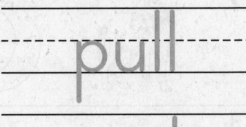 pull

2.     cook

3.   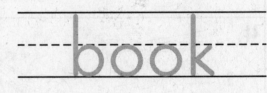 book

4.    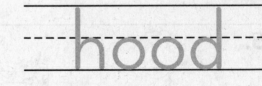 hood

5.     foot

6.     bush

Name _____

Write a word from the box to name each picture.

hood	brook	wood
bull	push	book

I.  _____

_____

2.  _____

_____

3. _____

_____

4.  _____

_____

5.  _____

_____

6.  _____

_____

Name _____

A. Read each word. Spell the words aloud. Then write the word.

1. after _____

2. buy _____

3. done _____

4. every _____

5. soon _____

6. work _____

B. Read each clue. Write a word from above to match it.

7. in a little while _____

8. spend cash _____

9. do a job _____

10. finished _____

Bill, Jill, and Phil went back
and munched on grass.
They ate and ate.
"Grass tastes best after
such a good game,"
said Bill.

High-Frequency Words:
Circle the words <u>soon</u>,
<u>work</u>, and <u>after</u> in
the story.

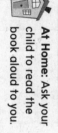

At Home: Ask your
child to read the
book aloud to you.

A Good Game

Bill, Jill, and Phil stood.
Soon they felt full.
Bill spoke. "We must run."

"Get set! Let's jump!"
When the pals stopped,
Jill said, "That's such a
good game."
"We must eat," said Phil.

Comprehension: What kind of game do
Bill, Jill, and Phil play?

They pulled and pushed a
log. It took lots of work.
It took a long time to get
the wood in place.

Phonics: Underline one word that rhymes
with pull. Underline three words that
rhyme with hood.

Name _____

Blend the sounds your teacher says to form a word. Circle the picture that shows the word.

Teacher Directions: Listen as I say the following sounds. Blend the sounds to say each word and then circle the picture that shows it. 1. /n/ /ā/ /l/; 2. /h/ /ā/; 3. /r/ /ā/ /n/; 4. /t/ /r/ /ā/; 5. /s/ /n/ /ā/ /l/

Name _____

 p<u>ai</u>l   pl<u>ay</u>

Say each picture name. Write the letters <u>ai</u> or <u>ay</u> to complete each word.

1.    r_____n

2.    h_____

3.    tr_____

4.   p_____nt

5.   n_____l

Name _____

Say each picture name. Circle the word that names each picture.

1.

    man   mail

2.

    chain chin

3.

    sail   sand

4.

    trap   tray

5.

    play   plus

6.

    braid   brake

Name _____

A. Read each word. Then spell and trace the word.

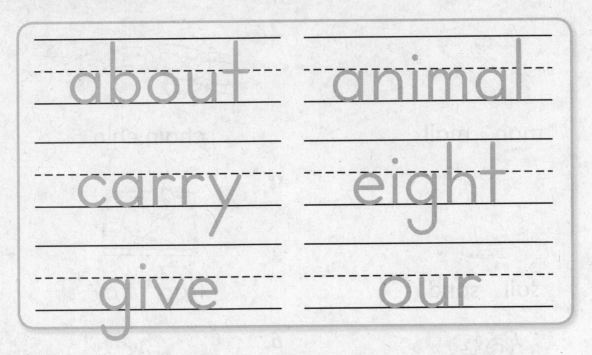

about   animal

carry   eight

give   our

B. Write a word to complete each sentence.

1. Here is _____ school.

2. The shape has _____ sides.

3. He will _____ the backpack.

4. This book is _____ chimps.

Gray smiles now.
"I will carry my flute.
It made Gray well,"
claims Kay.
"Playing did it," says Dad.

High-Frequency Words:
Circle the words about,
eight, and carry in
the story.

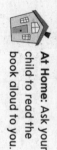

At Home: Ask your
child to read the
book aloud to you.

Gray the Mule

Kay's mule is named Gray.
On this day, Gray's tail
dips down. Gray is about
to trip and sway.
"Gray is in pain," says Kay.

Kay plays eight quick
tunes. Gray taps and brays.
Dad claps, "Gray likes that
playing, Kay."

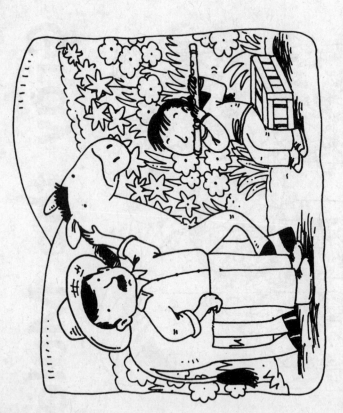

Kay says, "Wait here, Dad.
Stay with Gray."
Kay gets her flute and plays.
She explains, "This may
help Gray."

Name _____

Name the pictures in each row. Listen for the middle sound in each picture name. Circle the two pictures whose names have the same middle sound.

I.			

2.			

3.			

4.			

5.			

Name _____

teeth

Read each word. Circle the picture it names.

I. sheep

2. bean

3. tree

4. queen

5. seal

6. chief

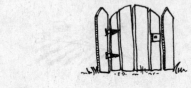

Name _____

Read each word in the box. Write the word under the picture whose name has the long <u>e</u> sound spelled the same way.

heat	keep	brief
dream	field	sweet

wh<u>ee</u>l   p<u>ea</u>ch   sh<u>ie</u>ld

_____   _____   _____

- - - - - - - - - - - - - -   - - - - - - - - - - - - - -   - - - - - - - - - - - - - -

_____   _____   _____

- - - - - - - - - - - - - -   - - - - - - - - - - - - - -   - - - - - - - - - - - - - -

_____   _____   _____

Name _____

A. Read each word. Then spell and trace the word.

1. 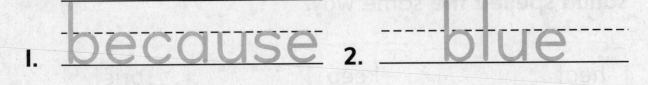 because

2. blue

3. into

4. or

5. other

6. small

B. Write a word from above to complete each sentence.

7. I dive _____ the blue water.

8. This _____ cat is small.

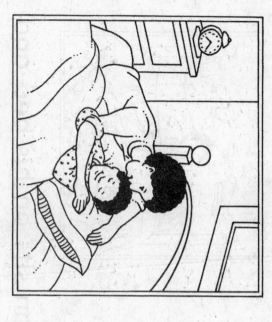

Kean gets into bed
between his sheets. Mom
hugs Kean. "That's just
what I needed," says Kean.
"Sweet dreams, Kean,"
says Mom.

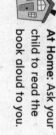

Sleep for Kean

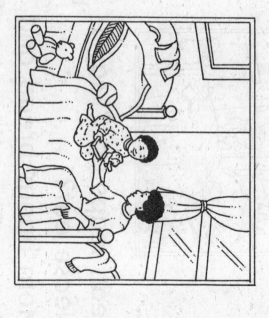

Kean can not sleep.
His new bed is not like his
other bed.
"Please read to me,"
says Kean.
Mom reads, then says,
"Sleep, Kean."

①

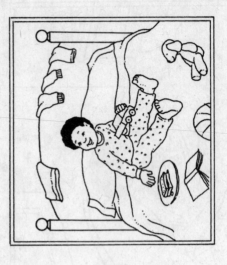

Kean sits on his bed and plays. He says, "I can't sleep because I need one last thing." "What can it be?" asks Mom.

Comprehension: Why can't Kean sleep?

Kean leaps up. "May I please eat?" Mom brings bread and cheese. Then Kean brushes his teeth. "Please sleep, Kean," says Mom.

Phonics: Draw a line under two words with long e spelled e, two words with long e spelled ee, and two words with long e spelled ea.

Name _____

Name the pictures in each row. Listen for the middle sound in each picture name. Put X on the picture whose name has a different middle sound.

Name _____

b**oa**t   g**r**ow   c**o**ld

Read each word. Then spell and trace the word. Then draw a line from the word to the picture it names.

1.

2.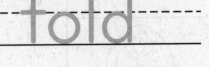

3.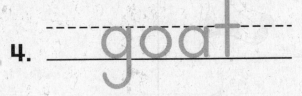

4.

5.

6.

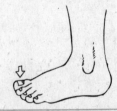

Name _____

Write a word from the box to name each picture.

cold	float	crow
toast	row	soap

1.
   _____
   - - - - - - - - - - - - - - -
   _____

2.
   _____
   - - - - - - - - - - - - - - -
   _____

3.
   _____
   - - - - - - - - - - - - - - -
   _____

4.
   _____
   - - - - - - - - - - - - - - -
   _____

5.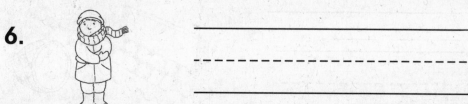
   _____
   - - - - - - - - - - - - - - -
   _____

6.
   _____
   - - - - - - - - - - - - - - -
   _____

Name _____

A. Read each word. Then spell and trace the word.

1. ____ find ____

2. ____ food ____

3. ____ more ____

4. ____ over ____

5. ____ start ____

6. ____ warm ____

B. Write a word from above that means the opposite.

7. not end _____

8. not under _____

9. not cold _____

10. not less _____

A plane is fast. It starts on land and travels up, over us. Planes make long trips seem quick. Which way is best?

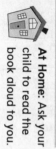
At Home: Ask your child to read the book aloud to you.

Comprehension: Which is the fastest way to go?

Ways to Go

How can we go? We can find many ways to go. Some are fast and some are slow.

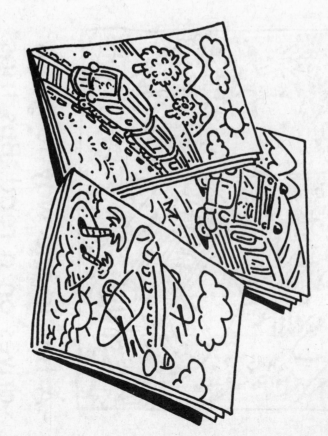

A train can go fast. It rides on a track. Trains make lots of stops. Trains can go at very fast speeds.

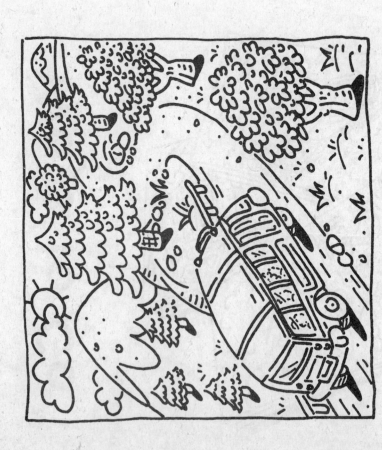

A bus is one way to go. It drives on a road. Bus trips can be quick, but a long trip on a bus may be slow.

Name_____

Name the pictures in each row. Circle the two pictures whose names have one sound that is the same.

Name _____

 night   fry   child   cries

Read each word. Circle the picture it names.

I. sky

2. tie

3. light

4. pie

5. fly

6. wind

Name _____

Read the word. Take away and add letters. Write the new word. Then draw a picture to show the word.

1. night – n + l = _____

2. wild – w + ch = _____

3. tie – t + p = _____
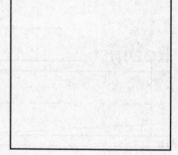

4. fry – r + l = _____
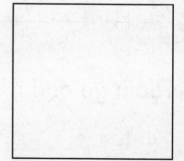

Name _____

A. Read each word. Then spell and trace the word.

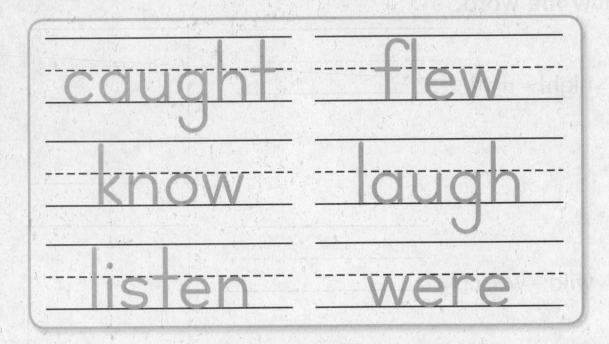

caught   flew

know   laugh

listen   were

B. Choose a word from above to complete each sentence in the story.

_____

Robins _____ flying. Jane

_____ one robin. She did not

_____ what to do. Then Jane let the

robin go and it _____ away.

Frog went right up the tree behind Dog. He helped Dog get Pig's kite.

Pig said, "I will fly my kite again thanks to my kind pals."

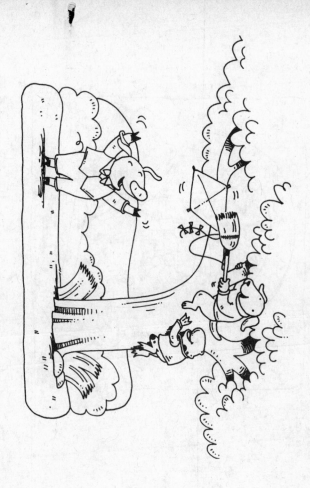

Comprehension: What should Pig do next time he flies his kite?

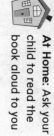
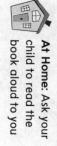

At Home: Ask your child to read the book aloud to you

Pig Flies His Kite

Pig sent his kite up. It flew high in the bright blue sky. What a nice sight!

Dog tried to reach the kite, but he could not get it. Frog spied Pig and Dog out his window. "Dog needs help," said Frog.

High-Frequency Words: Circle the words know, flew, and caught in the story.

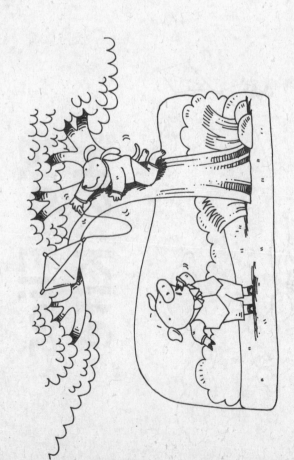

Then Pig's kite went into a tree. It got caught. "My kite!" cried Pig. "I know what to do," said Dog.

Phonics: Draw a line under two words with long *i* spelled *y*, two words with long *i* spelled *igh*, and two words with long *i* spelled *ie*.

Name _____

Name the pictures in each row. Listen for the end sound in each picture name. Put X on the picture whose name has a different ending sound.

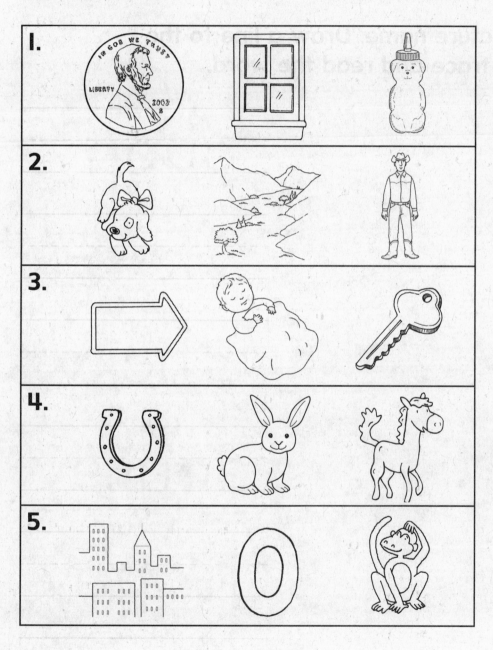

Name _____

 pony    **monkey**

Say each picture name. Draw a line to the word. Then trace and read the word.

1.

2.

3.

4.

5.

6.

puppy

key

sticky

donkey

trophy

funny

Name _____

Write the letters on the line to make a word. Read the word. Then circle the picture the word names.

_____

- - - - - - - - - - - - - - -

1. monk + ey _____

_____

- - - - - - - - - - - - - - -

2. wind + y _____

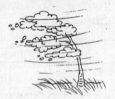   

_____

- - - - - - - - - - - - - - -

3. penn + y _____

_____

- - - - - - - - - - - - - - -

4. bab + y _____

_____

- - - - - - - - - - - - - - -

5. sunn + y _____

Name _____

A. Read each word. Then spell and trace each word.

1. 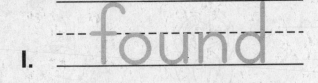 found

2.  hard

3.  near

4. woman

5. would

6. write

B. Draw a line from each word to its meaning.

7. found   use a pen

8. write   not easy

9. hard   not far

10. near   not lost

The monkeys set out peanuts.
This was a nice, nutty snack.
Then Lenny had to leave and
head home. But he would
visit his monkey pals again.

High-Frequency Words:
Circle the words near,
found, and would in
the story.

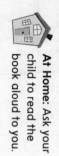

At Home: Ask your
child to read the
book aloud to you.

Monkeys in
a Tree

Lenny spotted a big tree
near his home. Lenny
checked the leaves. He had
not seen this kind of tree
any place else.

Up went Lenny. He did not
need keys.
Lenny was amazed! He
spotted two monkeys sitting
inside the cozy shack.

Comprehension: Why is Lenny surprised
to find monkeys in the shack?

Lenny went close to the
tree trunk. He found
steps leading up into its
branches. He looked up
and spied a shack sitting
high in the tree branches.

Phonics: Draw a line under the story
words with long e spelled y and ey.

Name _____

Say the picture name. Listen for the vowel sound. Then say the picture names in the same row. Put X on the picture whose name does not have the same vowel sound.

Name _____

jar

Read each word. Circle the picture it names.

1. chart

2. car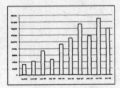

3. scarf

4. shark

5. barn

6. cart

Name _____

Say each picture name. Circle the pictures whose names have the vowel sound you hear in *car*. Write the letters *ar* to complete the picture name.

1.

_____

b _____ n

2.

_____

j _____

3.

_____

fr _____ g

4.

_____

f _____ m

5.

_____

st _____

6.

_____

p _____ k

Name _____

A. Read each word. Then spell and trace the word.

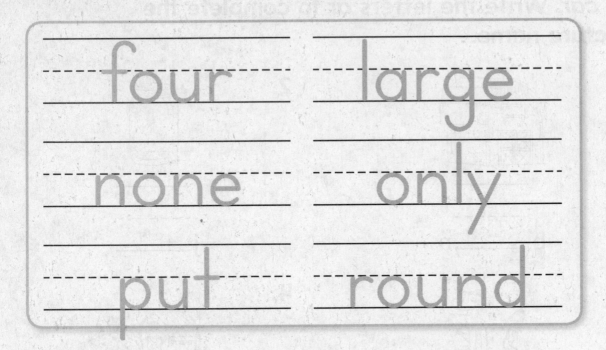

four   large

none   only

put   round

B. Choose words to complete each sentence.

1. _____ take away two is two.

2. The sun is a _____ star.

3. Please _____ the pen back in the box.

Then Mom, Dad, and Mark
went back.
"That is only one trail. Let's
try a new trail next week,"
said Mark.

High-Frequency Words:
Circle the words four, put,
and only in the story.

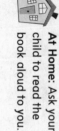

At Home: Ask your
child to read the
book aloud to you.

At the Park

Mom, Dad, and Mark went
hiking in the park. It had four
good trails. Which was the
best place to start?
Mom chose a good trail
for kids.

Mom, Dad, and Mark stopped at one part of the trail. This park was filled with animals. Dad looked far away. Mom looked up. Mark looked close by at a stump.

Comprehension: Why do you think Mark and his family enjoyed hiking in the park?

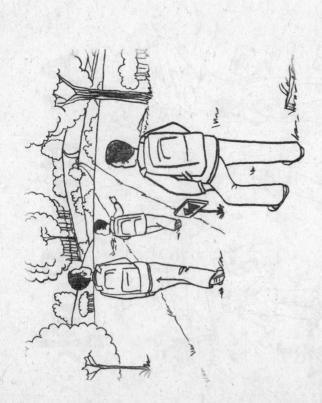

Mark put out his hand and led the way. "It's not hard to hike on this flat trail," he noted. They hiked far on the easy trail.

Phonics: Underline words in the story that have ar as in car.

Name _____

Say the picture name. Take away the first sound and say the new word. Circle the picture that shows it.

Name _____

 g**ir**l   w**or**m   h**er**b   c**ur**b

Say each picture name. Circle the word that names each picture.

1.   bird
                          bed

2.    pass
                          purse

3.    hood
                          herd

4.    worm
                          wood

5.    shirt
                          sheet

6.  fan
                          fern

Name _____

Write a word from the box to name each picture.

perch	thirty	world
burn	nurse	skirt

1.

_____

- - - - - - - - - - - - - - - - - -

_____

2.

_____

- - - - - - - - - - - - - - - - - -

_____

3.

_____

- - - - - - - - - - - - - - - - - -

_____

4.

_____

- - - - - - - - - - - - - - - - - -

_____

5.

_____

- - - - - - - - - - - - - - - - - -

_____

6.

_____

- - - - - - - - - - - - - - - - - -

_____

Name _____

A. Read, spell, and trace the word.

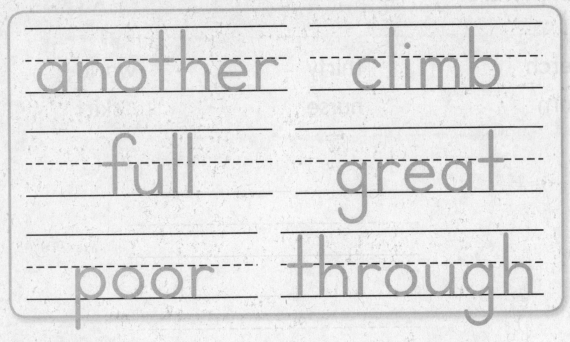

another   climb

full   great

poor   through

B. Write a word to complete each sentence.

1. Jess can _____ the tree.

2. This bank is _____ of pennies.

3. That was a really _____ show!

4. I would like _____ plum.

This black and white bird can not fly through the sky. It walks and slides on ice.

It is another bird with webbed feet. These help it swim in the sea.

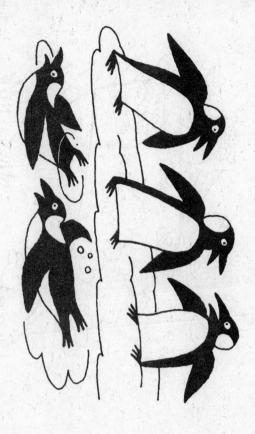

Comprehension: How do webbed feet help some birds?

At Home: Ask your child to read the book aloud to you.

A World of Birds

Ducks make homes in rivers, lakes, and ponds. Webbed feet help this bird swim. It dives under water to catch and eat plants, fish, and bugs.

This bird is a great hunter.
It sees well in the dark, so it
hunts at night.
This bird will perch on a
branch. Then it will turn to
catch a rabbit.

High-Frequency Words:
Circle the words great, through, and
another in the story.

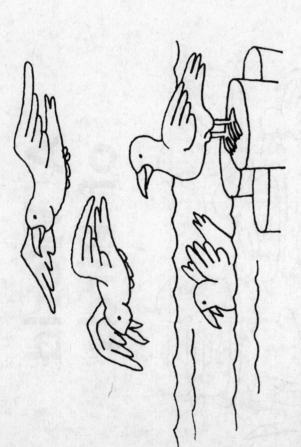

Sea gulls catch crabs and
fish to eat.
In winter, this bird flies to
escape cold weather.

Phonics: Underline the words in the story
that have the same vowel sound you hear
in her, sir, fur, and work.

Name _____

Say each picture name to yourself. Then add the sound at the beginning of the word *rose* to the beginning of each picture name. Circle the picture that names the new word.

Name _____

 corn   **chore**   **board**

Say each picture name. Draw a line to the word. Then trace and read the word.

1.

2.

3.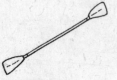

4.

5.

6.

core

horse

fork

porch

thorn

oar

Name _____

Read each word in the box. Write the word under the picture whose name has the vowel sound spelled the same way.

oar	more	north
cord	board	chore

h<u>or</u>n

st<u>ore</u>

s<u>oar</u>

_____

- - - - - - - - - - - - -

_____

_____

- - - - - - - - - - - - -

_____

Name _____

A. Read each word. Then trace and write the word.

1. 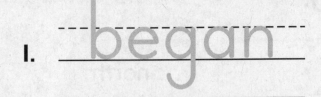 began

2.  better

3. 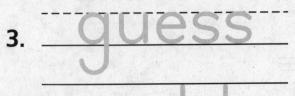 guess

4.  learn

5.  right

6.  sure

B. Write a word from above to complete each sentence.

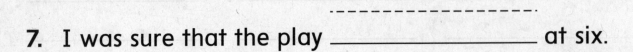

7. I was sure that the play _____ at six.

8. I learn the _____ way to type.

This sport is fun. Players pitch and catch. They hit with a bat to score.

Which sport is right for you?

Try all sorts of sports. Then you can be sure!

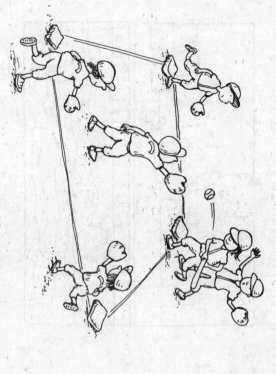

High-Frequency Words: Circle the words learn, right, and sure in the story.

At Home: Ask your child to read the book aloud to you.

Learn a Sport

Sports can be fun. Which sport is best? Pick a sport that you like. A coach can help you learn more about it.

Swimming is another fun sport. The coach shows swimmers how to jump off the board and swim. Swimmers swim back and forth. The coach times each lap.

Comprehension: What kinds of equipment do people use for sports?

Riding a bike is a fun sport. Use a helmet, and ride with a pal. Bike riders can race for long distances or on short tracks.

Phonics: Underline words in the story that have the same vowel sound you hear in fork, chore, and roar.

Name _____

Say the picture name. Listen for the middle sound. Say each picture name below. Put a ✓ in the box for each picture name that has the same middle sound.

Name _____

<u>ow</u>l   r<u>ou</u>nd

Read each word. Circle the picture it names.

1. mouse

2. cloud

3. clown

4. plow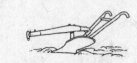

5. house

6. crown

Name _____

Say each picture name. Write the letters *ou* or *ow* to complete each word.

1. h_____se

2. cl_____n

3. d_____n

4. c_____ch

5. m_____se

6. c_____

Name _____

A. Read each word. Then spell and trace the word.

1.  color

2.  early

3.  instead

4.  nothing

5.  oh

6.  thought

B. Write a word from above to complete each sentence.

7. Tim  _____, "Oh! I will get a pet."

8. It is too early to take the bus, so I will

walk _____.

The man agreed to help. He gave Jack ten bags of gold. "Thanks," said Jack.

The huge man and Jack looked down at the lucky town from the clouds.

High-Frequency Words:

At Home: Ask your child to read the book aloud to you.

Circle the words <u>early</u>, <u>thought</u>, and <u>instead</u> in the story.

Jack Helps His Town

Early one morning, Jack planted beans in the ground. A big plant rose up into the clouds. Jack went up this thick vine. He could see his whole town.

Jack did not go, but said,
"I see so much gold. My
town needs help. We need
cows and plows. We need
to fix houses. Will you help
us, please?"

Comprehension: Why does Jack ask the
man for help?

Jack reached the top. He
thought he would just see
more clouds.
Instead, Jack found a huge
man counting out his gold.
The man shouted, "How did
you get up top? Get out now!"

Phonics: Underline words in the story that
have the same vowel sound you hear in
mouse and **brown**.

Name _____

Listen as your teacher reads the directions.

Teacher Directions: Listen as I say the following sounds. Blend the sounds to say a word and then circle the picture that shows it. 1. /b/ /oi/ /l/; 2. /t/ /oi/ /z/; 3. /k/ /oi/ /n/ /z/; 4. /b/ /oi/; 5. /p/ /oi/ /n/ /t/

Name _____

boil

toy

Say each picture name. Circle the pictures whose names have the vowel sound you hear in <u>boil</u>. Write *oy* or *oi* to complete the picture name.

1.

_____

s_____l

2.

_____

t_____s

3.

_____

c_____ns

4.

_____

j_____

5.

_____

p_____nt

6.

_____

b_____

Name _____

Read each word in the box. Write the word under the picture whose name has the vowel sound spelled the same way.

join	toy	foil
spoil	soy	joy

b<u>oy</u>   p<u>oi</u>nt

1. _____

2. _____

3. _____

4. _____

5. _____

6. _____

Name _____

A. Read each word. Spell the words as you trace the letters.

1.

2.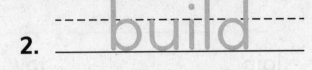

3.

4.

5.

6.

B. Fill in the blanks using words from above. Use the clues to help you.

7. trip _____

8. cash _____

9. on top of _____

10. put together _____

Morning came. The sun rose above the sill. Could the toys slip back in Roy's toy chest? The toys got in. And the lid shut for another day.

High-Frequency Words:
Circle the words toward, knew, and above in the story.

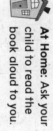

Toy Time

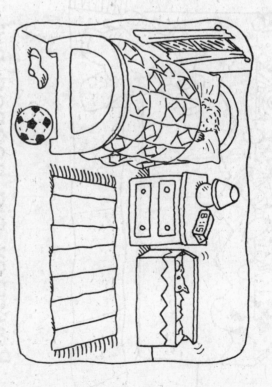

Roy enjoyed playing with his toys. At night, Roy put his toys in his toy chest, and went to sleep. What was that noise? The lid of Roy's toy chest creaked open.

The toys skipped. Pig led
the way.
"This is fun," said the boy
and girl dolls in low voices.
"I'll play all night,"
chuckled Pig with joy.

Comprehension: What do the toys do
after they get out of the toy chest?

Roy's toy pig hopped out
of the chest. Pig waved
toward the other toys.
They knew it was play
time. They joined Pig.

Phonics: Draw a line under words with oy
and oi.

Name _____

Name the pictures in each row. Circle the two pictures whose names have one sound that is the same. Say the sound.

Name _____

Say each picture name. Draw a line to the word. Then trace and read the word.

1.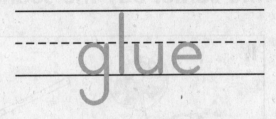

2.

3.

4.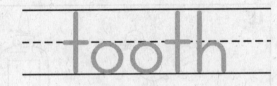

5.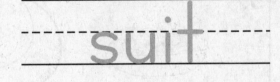

6.

Name _____

Say each picture name. Circle the word that names each picture.

I.

goose   gas

2.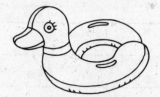

tub   tube

3.

fruit   frog

4.

glow   glue

5.

chat   chew

6.

juice   junk

Name _____

A. Read each word. Then spell and trace the word.

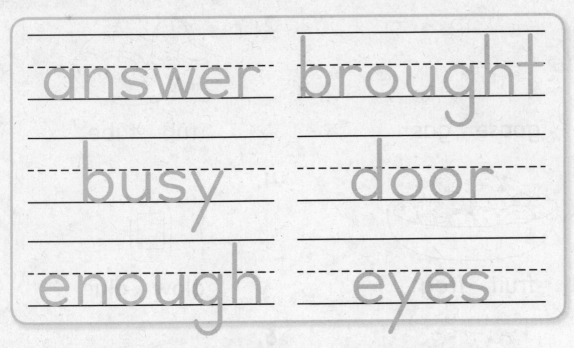

B. Read the story. Choose a word from above to complete each sentence in the story.

There was a knock at my _____. I went

to _____ it. My _____ grew

big. My pal had _____ me a huge bunch

of flowers!

Ruth's eyes lit up. "I think I know. Are we getting a dog?" she asked.

Dad replied, "Yes. You can choose the dog's name."

"I will name it Pancake," said Ruth.

High-Frequency Words:
Circle the words <u>answer</u>, <u>brought</u>, and <u>eyes</u> in the story.

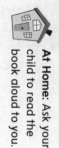

At Home: Ask your child to read the book aloud to you.

Clues from Dad

Ruth woke up and smelled pancakes. That put her in a good mood. Pancakes were Dad's good news food.

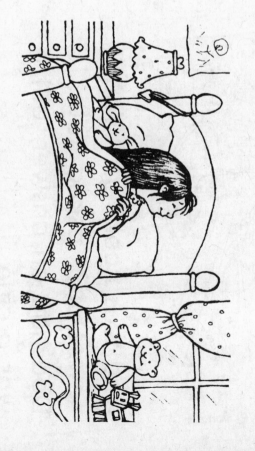

Dad brought out a plate
with bits of pancake on it.
It looked like a puzzle.
"Here is another clue, Ruth,"
said Dad. Ruth smiled.

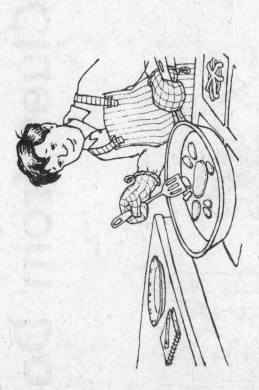

Dad was cooking. "What's
new, Dad?" asked Ruth.
Dad had an answer, but it
was a clue.
"You will be getting a
surprise soon. You can pet it
and cuddle it, too," said Dad.

Name _____

Name the pictures in each row. Listen for the vowel sound in each picture name. Put X on the picture whose name has a different vowel sound.

Name _____

w**all**	w**a**sp	cr**aw**l	h**au**l

Read each word. Circle the picture it names.

1. fawn

2. walk

3. salt

4. ball

5. claw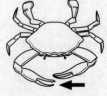

6. caught

Name _____

Write a word from the box to name each picture.

haul	chalk	wall
saw	crawl	talk

1.  _____

2.  _____

3.  _____

4. _____

5.  _____

6.  _____

Name _____

A. Read each word. Trace each word as your spell the word.

1.

2.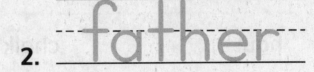

3.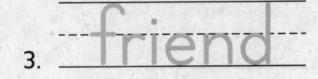

4.

5.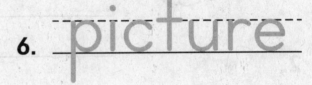

6. picture

B. Use the words from above to complete the sentences.

7. Another word for <u>mom</u> is _____.

8. Another word for <u>pal</u> is _____.

9. Another word for <u>photo</u> is _____.

A cat always licks its paws after it eats. It licks its fur, too. That's because a cat is a very clean animal. A cat likes clean paws and claws.

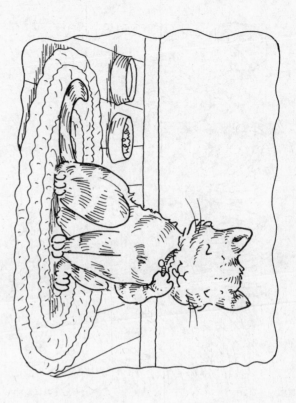

High-Frequency Words: Circle the words love, friend, and picture in the story.

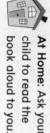

At Home: Ask your child to read the book aloud to you.

Paws and Claws

People love cats. A cat can be a best friend. A cat needs looking after. If a cat hurts its paw, a vet can take an x-ray picture. She will check the cat's claws, too.

A cat crawls in the tall
grass to hunt. Its claws
will help it catch food.
Once the food is caught,
the cat brings it home.

Comprehension: How can a cat use
its claws?

A cat's claws are sharp.
Sharp claws help a cat
walk up a tree trunk.
If the cat halts at the
top, it may get stuck.
Then the cat will need
some help getting down.

Phonics: Draw a line under words that
have the same vowel sound you hear
in saw.

Name _____

Say the picture name. Listen for the beginning sound. Then say the picture names in the same row. Put X on the picture whose name does not have the same beginning sound.

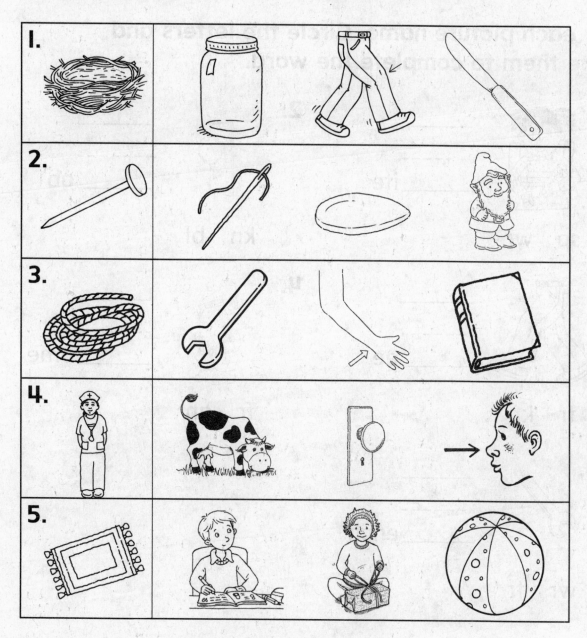

Name _____

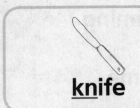
knife

gnat

wrist

Say each picture name. Circle the letters and write them to complete the word.

1.

_____
- - - - - - -
_____ite

sp   wr

2.

_____
- - - - - - -
_____ob

kn   bl

3.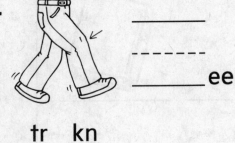

_____
- - - - - - -
_____ee

tr   kn

4.

_____
- - - - - - -
_____ome

fr   gn

5.

_____
- - - - - - -
_____ench

wr   tr

Say each picture name. Circle the word that names each picture.

1.

knot   not

2.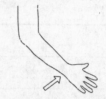

wrist   risk

3.

gnat   note

4.

night   knife

5.

rap   wrap

6.

knit   nit

Name _____

A. Read each word. Then spell and trace the word.

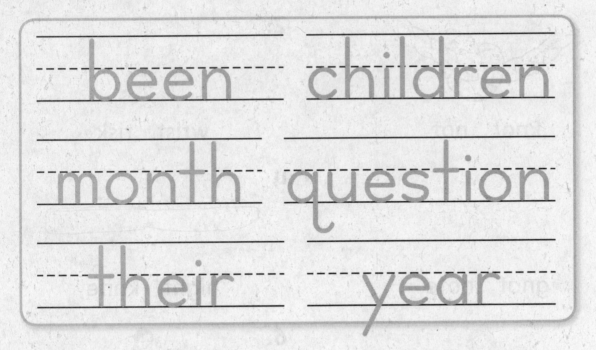

been   children

month   question

their   year

B. Write a word from above to complete each sentence.

1. Lee has a _____ for her teacher.

2. Have you _____ to the park?

3. There are twenty _____ in their class.

Know How to Slide

Ruby and Rob put on knit caps and mittens. They wrap scarves around their necks. They button up their coats. It's the time of the year to play in snow. Rob knows how to slide.

Ruby and Rob take one last slide. Then their day in the snow is done. It has been lots of fun sliding on snow. Now it's time to go inside and get warm. Ruby and Rob can slide another day.

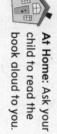

At Home: Ask your child to read the book aloud to you.

High-Frequency Words: Circle the words year, their, and been in the story.

Rob watches Ruby slide. He taught her how to slide right. He knows Ruby will stay safe on snow.

Comprehension: How do you think Ruby and Rob feel about sliding on snow?

Ruby slides in the snow. She knows how to slide right. She will not slide the wrong way.

Phonics: Underline words with wr and kn.

Name _____

Listen as your teacher reads the directions.

1.		
2.		
3		
4		
5.		

Teacher Directions: Say the first picture name. Say the sound /sh/. Add /sh/ to the beginning of *rug* and say the new word. Then circle the picture that shows it. Repeat with the following: 2. /st/, ring; 3. /th/, row; 4. /sp/, ray; 5. /b/, lock.

Name _____

string

three

scrap

Say each picture name. Draw a line to the word. Then trace and read the word.

1.

spray

2.

splash

3.

scratch

4.

street

5.

shrimp

6.

throne

Name _____

Write the letters on the line to make a word. Read the word. Then circle the picture the word names.

_____

----

1. spl + it _____

_____

----

2. thr + ee _____

_____

----

3. str + ong _____

_____

----

4. scr + ub _____

_____

----

5. spr + ing _____

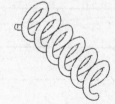

Name _____

A. Read each word. Then spell and trace the word.

1. 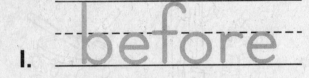 before

2. 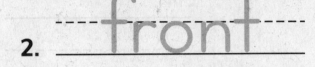 front

3.  heard

4.  push

5.  tomorrow

6. 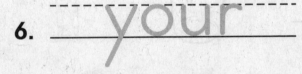 your

B. Write the word from above that means the opposite.

7. back _____

8. after _____

I call, "It's time for your bath, Scruff!"
Scruff jumps in the tub and I scrub him clean.
He splashes so we both get wet. When we dry off, we'll play some more.

High-Frequency Words:
Circle the words <u>front</u>, <u>push</u>, and <u>your</u> in the story.

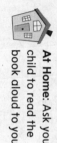

At Home: Ask your child to read the book aloud to you.

In the Spring

In the spring, I run outside with my dog Scruff. I run in front and Scruff follows me. We like to splash in the puddles.

Next, we make three big
flags. My flag has stripes.
Tim's flag has lines and
Patty's kite has spots.
Our three flags wave in
the strong breeze. Scruff
has a tiny flag to carry!

Scruff and I meet three
friends. My friends and I
fly kites on strings.
The wind can push our
kites high. Our kites
streak across the sky. It's
thrilling to see them fly.